P9-DEQ-379

Think Like a Computer

JACOB BATCHELOR

Children's Press®
An Imprint of Scholastic Inc.

Content Consultant

Sarah Otts, Scratch Online Community Developer, MIT Media Lab

Library of Congress Cataloging-in-Publication Data
Names: Batchelor, Jacob, author.
Title: Think like a computer / by Jacob Batchelor.
Description: North Mankato, MN : Children's Press, an imprint of Scholastic Inc., 2019. | Series: A true book | Includes bibliographical references and index.
Identifiers: LCCN 2018023823| ISBN 9780531127315 (library binding) | ISBN 9780531135402 (pbk.)
Subjects: LCSH: Computers—Juvenile literature. | Computer systems—Juvenile literature. | Computer programming—Juvenile literature.
Classification: LCC QA76.23 .B376 2019 | DDC 004—dc23
LC record available at https://lccn.loc.gov/2018023823

SCHOLASTIC, CHILDREN'S PRESS, A TRUE BOOK™, and associated logos are trademarks and/or registered trademarks of Scholastic Inc.

Scholastic Inc., 557 Broadway, New York, NY 10012

1 2 3 4 5 6 7 8 9 10 R 28 27 26 25 24 23 22 21 20 19

Front: Young programmers
Back: Apps

Find the Truth!

Everything you are about to read is true *except* for one of the sentences on this page.

Which one is **TRUE**?

T or F There are about a dozen different programming languages.

T or F A computer's physical parts are called hardware.

Find the answers in this book.

3

Contents

THE **BIG** TRUTH!

Artificial Intelligence

Ada Lovelace

There are millions of apps available today.

4 The Future of Computers

How can computers improve
everyday household devices?

This is Ralphie. Help him on page 42!

There are more than 4 billion internet users around the world today.

CHAPTER 1

The Age of Computers

How many times per day do you use a computer? Once? Twice? Three times? Chances are good that you use computers a lot more than you think. You probably use a laptop, tablet, or phone to surf the internet, watch videos, or chat with friends every day. But there are also computers in many cars, household appliances, and other everyday devices. We live in an age of computers, and it's important to understand how they work.

What Is a Computer?

Today, we think of computers as electronic devices. But the word *computer* dates back to at least the 1600s—long before humans learned to control electricity. *Computer* means "one who calculates." A computer is any device that can carry out a task automatically. An early example of a computer was the abacus. This device helped people count and perform math calculations by moving beads on a simple frame. Later, human "computers" were hired to analyze data for the military and other groups.

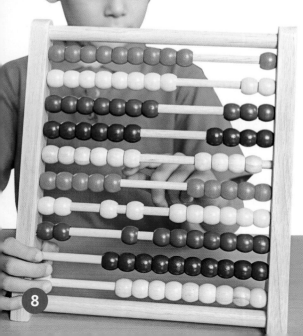

There are many types of abacuses. Different colors of beads often stand for different amounts. For example, orange beads might count as 10, while yellow ones count as 100.

The first self-driving cars were built in the 1980s.

All new cars produced today contain computer systems.

In more recent years, computers have become capable of much more than simple calculations. They guide planes, tanker ships, and cars to their destinations. They can help you research the answers to life's biggest questions or help you find the funniest cat video of all time. Each year, new technology enables computers to take on more exciting and complicated tasks.

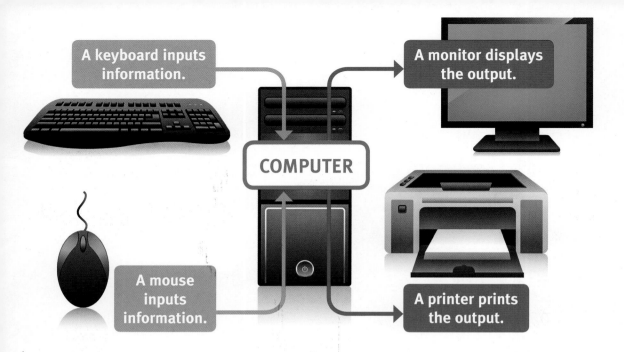

A keyboard inputs information.

A monitor displays the output.

COMPUTER

A mouse inputs information.

A printer prints the output.

Modern Computing

Computers come in all shapes and sizes. They carry out all sorts of different tasks. But almost all computers have the same basic structure. There are devices, such as a mouse or keyboard, that let you give information to a computer. This information is called **input**. The computer processes input, stores data, and delivers information called **output**. Devices such as screens and printers display the output for a user to see.

Hardware

All the physical parts of the computer are called **hardware**. Hardware includes input devices, output devices, and the electronics that help computers process and store information. The central processing unit, or CPU, is the most important piece of hardware. It's often called the brain of the computer. Modern CPUs are usually contained on a single **microchip**.

Today, a microchip small enough to fit in the palm of your hand has more computing power than the historic ENIAC computer, which took up an entire room.

1946

Today

Software

Computers don't think for themselves. They require specific instructions for everything they do. The programs that provide these instructions are called **software**. Some software runs in the background and doesn't require input from the user. Other software—such as apps, video games, and the other programs you use regularly—are designed to take your input. All programs are created by teams of software developers.

There are more than two million different apps available on Apple's App Store.

Every app you use on a computer or other electronic device is created by programmers.

Ada Lovelace: The First Computer Programmer

In 1843, 27-year-old Ada Lovelace wrote an academic paper that described how computers might someday work. She argued that Charles Babbage's Analytical Engine, an early computing device, could do more than just math—it could even write music! In her paper, Lovelace included a computer program that the machine could use to calculate a series of numbers. As a result, she is often considered the world's first computer programmer.

Today, women only hold about one-quarter of all jobs in computing. Ada Lovelace Day, in October, celebrates Lovelace's work and encourages young women to study computer science.

The first modern programming languages were developed in the 1950s.

CHAPTER **2**

Talking to Computers

Did you know that computers have their own languages? These programming languages are for writing **code** and giving directions to computers. Like any written language, they use letters and numbers to communicate specific ideas. There are hundreds of different programming languages. Each has its own grammar and vocabulary, just like English, Spanish, or the other languages people speak to each other. Programmers use different languages for different tasks.

Programming Languages

Some programming languages are very adaptable. C, for example, is a general-purpose programming language that can be used in many different situations. JavaScript is another very useful language. It's used for writing internet-based programs. Most of the web pages you visit were written at least partially in JavaScript.

```
1    /* This line basically imports the "stdio" header file, part of
2     * the standard library. It provides input and output functionality
3     * to the program.
4     */
5    #include <stdio.h>
6
7    /*
8     * Function (method) declaration. This outputs "Hello, world" to
9     * standard output when invoked.
10    */
11   void sayHello() {
12       // printf() in C outputs the specified text (with optional
13       // formatting options) when invoked.
14       printf("Hello, world!");
15   }
16
17   /*
18    * This is a "main function". The compiled
19    * program will run the code defined here.
20    */
21   void main() {
22       // Invoke the sayHello() function.
23       sayHello();
24   }
```

This is code written in C. It's designed to output the text, "Hello, world!"

Because computers are used for so many different things, more and more specialized programming languages are always being created.

Other programming languages are more specialized. They have features that make them more efficient at certain tasks. For example, many engineers use a language called MATLAB. This language makes it easy to do complex mathematical calculations. When no existing language works well for a certain task, computer scientists often create new ones. This means programmers always have new things to learn, no matter how experienced they are.

Believe it or not, the right series of "on" and "off" switches can be used to create even the most complex computer programs.

Binary Code

Computers don't "understand" programming languages the same way humans do. They don't know what your commands mean. Instead, computers translate these commands into **binary** code. This is the most basic way computers receive and send information. Binary code is a pattern of 1s and 0s. 1 means "on." 0 means "off."

Computers are able to understand these 1s and 0s because of the way microchips work. These chips contain tiny electrical **circuits**. In binary, 1 turns the electricity on. 0 turns the electricity off. How do those 1s and 0s add up to everything you can do on a computer? It's hard to imagine, but modern computer chips contain millions and millions of on and off switches. Together, they can carry out a dazzling array of commands.

The binary code for a complicated program like a video game could contain millions upon millions of 1s and 0s.

Algorithms

The purpose of most programming languages is to write code that carries out **algorithms**. Algorithms are a series of steps or rules that must be followed to complete a task. Take baking, for example. If you're hungry for cookies, you might find a recipe and follow its directions. Preheat the oven, measure the ingredients, mix the dough, place the dough on a sheet, and bake. The process only works if you have the right ingredients and you follow the instructions carefully in the right order.

Algorithms in computer programs follow the same basic idea. They solve complex problems by following

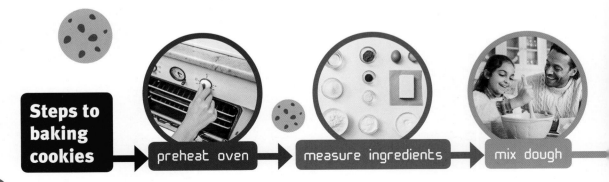

Steps to baking cookies → preheat oven → measure ingredients → mix dough

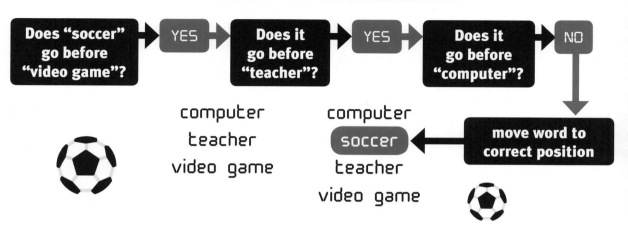

Algorithm to alphabetize words

Does "soccer" go before "video game"? → YES → Does it go before "teacher"? → YES → Does it go before "computer"? → NO

move word to correct position

computer
teacher
video game

computer
soccer
teacher
video game

programmed steps. Imagine you have a list of words on a computer that you need to alphabetize. An algorithm could look at each word in your list and determine whether it comes before or after the words next to it. Eventually, the algorithm would deliver an alphabetized list. This is called a sorting algorithm.

place on sheet → put in oven → cool/eat

THE BIG TRUTH!

Artificial Intelligence

Artificial intelligence (AI) programs can't think or feel in the same way humans do. But they are smart in other important ways. Today's AI programs are capable of machine learning. This means that the programs use large amounts of information to learn or to improve at a task. For example, Facebook's AI programs learn what you look like by looking at tagged pictures. Then, the programs can use this information to identify you in untagged photos.

AI is becoming more and more common. Here are a few areas in which the technology is making a difference:

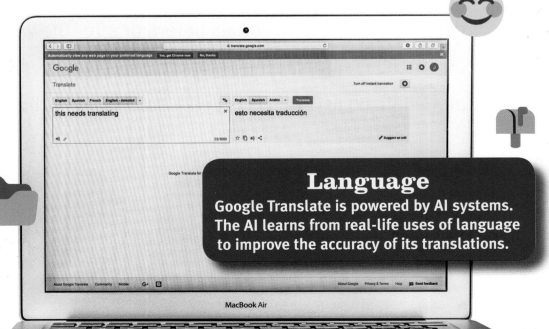

Language
Google Translate is powered by AI systems. The AI learns from real-life uses of language to improve the accuracy of its translations.

MacBook Air

Transportation

The future of self-driving cars depends on AI programs that can learn to make decisions quickly and drive like a human.

Health

AI systems can help doctors care for their patients by learning from medical records and suggesting treatment options.

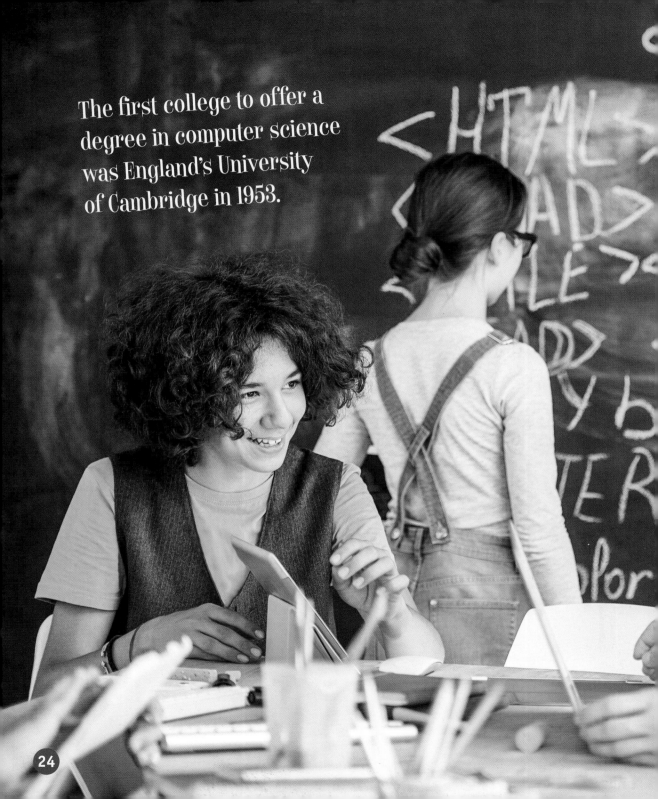

The first college to offer a degree in computer science was England's University of Cambridge in 1953.

CHAPTER 3

Writing (and Fixing) Code

You don't need any special training to start writing code. Once you begin, you will be a computer programmer! All you have to do is learn one of the many programming languages available and start trying it out. But it's important to remember that learning a new language takes time. You're guaranteed to make some mistakes along the way. Learning how to fix them is what counts.

Squashing Bugs

In coding, a "bug" is not an insect. It's a problem that needs to be fixed. You may remember that computer programs rely on algorithms, which follow a step-by-step process. Remember the example of an algorithm for baking cookies? You might run into a bug if the recipe was missing a step or if the recipe accidentally said "tablespoon" instead of "teaspoon." In either case, the cookies wouldn't come out right.

Even the best programmers end up with bugs in their programs sometimes. Everyone makes mistakes. So when a new computer program

What if you missed one of the steps to baking cookies, how would the cookies turn out? Go back to page 20 to find the mistake in this code.

Steps to baking cookies → preheat oven → measure ingredients

Debugging can be frustrating, but it is often a crucial part of creating a good program.

crashes, computer scientists usually don't get mad— they start debugging. Debugging is the process of searching through the code of a computer program to find mistakes. Once the problem is found and corrected, the computer program will hopefully run more smoothly. However, the process might take hours, days, or even longer!

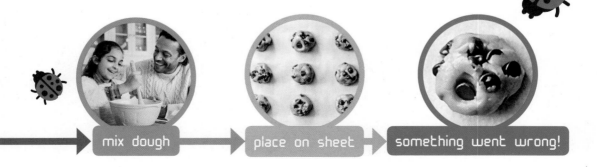

mix dough → place on sheet → something went wrong!

Getting a Virus

You may have heard that viruses are responsible for illnesses like the flu. They get inside you and use your body's cells to reproduce. But did you know that computers can get viruses, too? A computer virus is software that is designed to sneak into your computer and cause problems. Some of those problems include stealing your information or causing your computer to shut down.

Getting infected with a virus can cause major problems, from the loss of important files to theft of your personal information.

In 2018, Facebook founder Mark Zuckerberg was asked to testify before Congress after the personal data of millions of Facebook users was stolen by hackers.

Viruses can spread in many ways. Sometimes, people send them over the internet. These viruses can be hidden in links or email attachments. People called **hackers** use these viruses and other methods to access people's computers without permission. They can even use internet-connected devices, like cameras or TVs, to launch large attacks that can shut down websites or businesses. These attacks can cost companies millions of dollars and invade individuals' privacy.

Keeping Your Computer Safe

Sometimes bugs open up cracks in a program's security, allowing hackers to gain access. Other times, hackers use special software that can guess the passwords of computer users. Most computer security experts agree that there's no such thing as a perfectly safe computer. Modern computers are complex machines that run millions of lines of code at once. But don't worry—there are some easy ways to prevent most viruses and hacks.

CHECKLIST
What does a password need to be safe?

- ☐ A capital letter
- ☐ A lower case letter
- ☐ A number
- ☐ A symbol
- ☐ More than 12 characters
- ☐ Do not use your name
- ☐ Do not use your pet's name, especially if you posted its photos on social media
- ☐ Do not use a dictionary word
- ☐ Do not use your address
- ☐ Do not use your date of birth
- ☐ Change it every 3 months

Hackers use software that can guess as many as 8 million passwords a second!

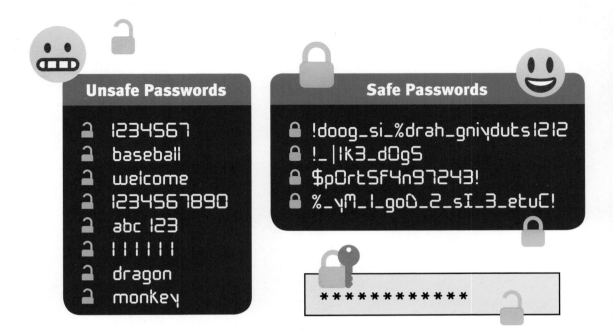

Unsafe Passwords
- 1234567
- baseball
- welcome
- 1234567890
- abc 123
- 111111
- dragon
- monkey

Safe Passwords
- !doog_si_%drah_gniyduts!212
- !_|Ik3_dOgS
- $pOrtSF4n97243!
- %_yM_I_goD_2_sI_3_etuC!

****

First, make sure to create strong passwords. Strong passwords have numbers, letters, and symbols and are hard to guess. "MniJ1089!" is a strong password. "Password123" isn't. Strong passwords are tougher for hackers to crack. Second, make sure to always update your software. Software developers create updates to fix bugs that could allow hackers to access your computer. Lastly, don't click on suspicious email attachments or visit unfamiliar websites.

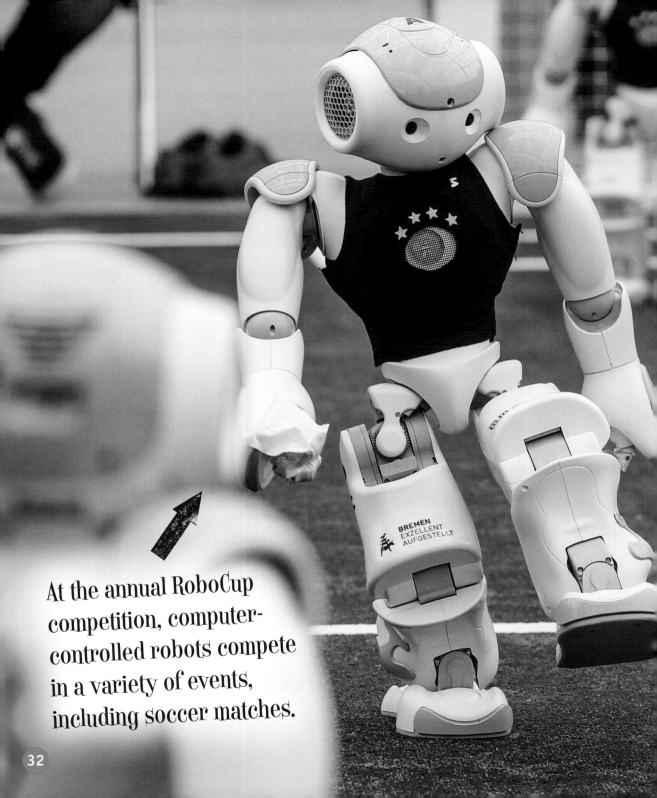

At the annual RoboCup
competition, computer-
controlled robots compete
in a variety of events,
including soccer matches.

The Future of Computers

Decades ago, few people would have predicted that computers would become such an essential part of everyday life. What will our lives be like 50 years from now? Will we still have computers as we know them? Or will our laptops and smartphones be replaced by new types of technology that we can't yet imagine? Only time will tell.

Smart Objects

One trend in computer technology today is the spread of "smart" objects. You're likely familiar with smartphones. But have you watched a smart TV or used a smart refrigerator? These devices contain computers that allow them to connect to the internet and communicate with other devices. In the future, it's likely that more and more everyday objects will contain powerful computers.

Timeline: Computers Through the Ages

1822
Charles Babbage designs a steam-powered machine capable of advanced calculations. It was never finished.

1939
Alan Turing and his team construct an electronic code-breaking machine (pictured) that helps pave the way for future computers.

1822 ▶ **1843** ▶ **1939** ▶ **1946** ▶

1843
Ada Lovelace, a collaborator of Babbage's, creates the first computer program.

1946
Researchers unveil ENIAC, an early computer that filled up a large room.

The Internet of Things

Many smart devices can connect to the internet. A smart TV can connect to online streaming services. Internet-enabled lights and security cameras can be controlled from a smartphone. Together, these interconnected machines are often called the Internet of Things. They can make life more convenient, but they could also present new targets for hackers.

1996
Sergey Brin and Larry Page create the Google search engine.

Today
Wearable computers and devices connected to the Internet of Things are becoming more and more popular.

1950s	1996	2007	Today

1950s
Grace Hopper creates the first programming language to use plain English words.

2007
The first iPhone is released, putting miniature computers into the hands of millions of people.

Wearable Computers

Since the invention of smartphones, many people have gotten used to carrying a computer with them at all times. But as computer chips get smaller and more powerful, it has become possible to wear computers, too. For example, smartwatches can connect with a phone to display text messages on your wrist. They can also keep track of your heartbeat and how much you exercise. Someday soon, even our clothes might contain computers.

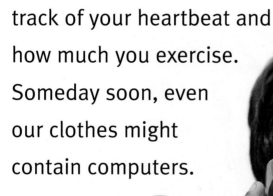

Google Glass is a wearable computer that users could control using head movements, voice commands, and touch.

The Thunderbird supercomputer is located at Sandia National Laboratories in New Mexico. It helps researchers predict how new weapons technology will perform in different environments.

Supercomputers

Supercomputers are able to process much more information than an average computer. These machines are generally used for modeling complex systems such as Earth's climate, ocean currents, or black holes. Computer engineers are working on a new generation of supercomputers, called quantum computers. If successful, these new computers could perform previously unimaginable feats, such as creating a digital version of a human brain.

The Good and Bad

Computers have made our lives better in many ways. They allow us to create new inventions, connect with people around the world, and spread information. But they also come with a cost. Some inventions encourage us to waste time. We sometimes prefer to connect online instead of in person. And information that we store on computers can be stolen. It's up to each new generation of computer engineers and everyday users to make use of computers responsibly and productively. 😃

While you should have fun with your computer and other devices, always keep safety in mind.

Computer Jobs

If you're interested in making a career out of computers, here are some jobs you might consider:

HARDWARE ENGINEER
Are you more interested in hardware? Hardware engineers design and build computer parts.

COMPUTER PROGRAMMER
Programmers write all kinds of software using different programming languages.

WEB DEVELOPER
If you love surfing the internet, becoming a web developer may be for you. These programmers create and maintain websites.

SECURITY SPECIALIST
These computer superheroes prevent hackers from accessing your information.

VIDEO GAME DESIGNER
That's right—video games need coders, too! Use your programming skills to build new worlds.

Write in (Binary) Code!

In this activity, you'll learn how to write in American Standard Code for Information Interchange, or ASCII. This binary code uses a series of 1s and 0s to represent letters, numbers, and symbols.

Step 1

Your computer uses ASCII to translate the letters you type on a keyboard into code. This chart shows how the letters of the alphabet are represented in ASCII. Look over the chart. Do you see any patterns?

ASCII BINARY ALPHABET

A	1000001	N	1001110
B	1000010	O	1001111
C	1000011	P	1010000
D	1000100	Q	1010001
E	1000101	R	1010011
F	1000110	S	1010011
G	1000111	T	1010100
H	1001000	U	1010101
I	1001001	V	1010110
J	1001010	W	1010111
K	1001011	X	1011011
L	1001100	Y	1011001
M	1001101	Z	1011010

1001000
1001001

1001100
1000101
1000001
1001000

Step 2

Get a piece of paper and a pencil. Use the chart on the left to write out your name or a secret message in ASCII.

Step 3

Once you've written your code, take it to a friend. Show your friend the ASCII chart and ask him or her to decode your message.

Think About It!

You wrote your code and gave it to a friend to translate. How was this similar to how a computer works?

41

Programming

Ralphie

How many different
routes to the school
bus can you create
using code?

In this activity, you'll use programming
skills to help Ralphie get to school. The
symbols in the box below represent
computer code. Use these symbols as
commands to get Ralphie from his starting
point to the school bus in the fewest
steps possible. Be sure to watch
out for obstacles. You don't want
Ralphie to run into a building!

CODE

▶ ◀ ▲ ▼

COMMANDS (or code meaning)

▶ Move one square right
◀ Move one square left
▲ Move one square up
▼ Move one square down

On a separate piece of paper, create another obstacle course for Ralphie to navigate. Challenge a friend to code Ralphie's new route.

Go Further!

43

True Statistics

Weight of the first portable computer: 30 lb. (13.6 kg)

Weight of an average laptop today: 3–5 lb. (1.4–2.3 kg)

Average salary of a computer programmer: $82,240 per year

Size of the smallest computer ever made: 0.04 in. by 0.04 in. (1 mm by 1 mm)

Number of worldwide internet users in 2018: More than 4 billion

Number of smartphones sold worldwide in 2017: 1.5 billion

Percent of U.S. school districts with internet access: 94

Number of letters, numbers, and symbols in ASCII: 255

Did you find the truth?

F There are about a dozen different programming languages.

T A computer's physical parts are called hardware.

Resources

Books

Briggs, Jason. *Python for Kids: A Playful Introduction to Programming*. San Francisco: No Starch Press, 2013.

Liukas, Linda. *Hello Ruby: Journey Inside the Computer*. New York: Feiwel and Friends, 2017.

Lyons, Heather. *Kids Get Coding* series. Minneapolis: Lerner Publications, 2017–2018.

Woodcock, Jon. *Coding Games in Scratch*. New York: DK Publishing, 2016.

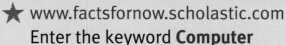

Visit this Scholastic website for more information on Thinking Like a Computer:
★ www.factsfornow.scholastic.com
Enter the keyword **Computer**

Important Words

algorithms (AL-guh-rih-thuhmz) processes or series of steps a computer can follow to complete a specific task

artificial intelligence (ahr-tuh-FISH-uhl in-TEL-ih-juhns) the science of making computers do things that previously needed human intelligence, such as understanding language

binary (BYE-nur-ee) in computers, binary refers to files and codes that convert all numbers and letters into strings of 1s and 0s

circuits (SUR-kits) complete paths for electrical currents

code (KODE) the instructions of a computer program, written in a programming language

hackers (HAK-urz) people who have special skills for getting into computer systems without permission

hardware (HAHRD-wair) computer equipment, such as a printer, monitor, or keyboard

input (IN-put) information fed into a computer

microchip (MYE-kroh-chip) a very thin piece of material that contains electrical circuits, used in computers and other electronic equipment

output (OUT-put) the information a computer produces

software (SAWFT-wair) computer programs that control the workings of the equipment, or hardware, and direct it to do specific tasks

Index

Page numbers in **bold** indicate illustrations.

About the Author

Jacob Batchelor studied English and creative writing at Dartmouth College in New Hampshire, and he currently writes and edits science-focused stories for Scholastic's *Science World*. When he's not hanging out in the library or writing books for kids, he likes to take long walks in Prospect Park near his home in Brooklyn, New York.